The Mad Knight and the Blue Stone

Epic Poems in the High Fantasy tradition

By

Steven Dufour

(The "C" in Celebrier's name is pronounced like a "K" as in Tolkien's Elvish.)

"I laugh at myself," said the quick-witted Elf.

"When I look myself in the eye.

Freedom, I think, is a very strong drink,

For all those who drink it die."

The Mad Knight

Chapter 1: The Situation

There was a Knight who once went mad.

And that, you will see, was very bad.

His madness made him terribly strong.

No one who opposed him lasted for long.

Celebrier was a boy who worked in the stables.

His dad worked there too. Mom waited on tables.

His special friend was his pet lizard,

Who, unknown to him, was a shape-shifting Wizard.

Celebrier dreamed it was his turn to fight.

He was the one who could conquer the Knight.

This worried his dad, who had fought in the wars,

So he took extra care to keep watch on his sword.

He said: "You wrestle with the other boys

And shoot at rabbits with your toys.

But such things would never work

Against a Knight who's gone berserk.

"You think you are David with his sling and his stone

Or else Saint George who faced a Dragon alone.

But you need more time to become big and strong

So safe here at home is where you belong."

Late that night Celebrier crept

To his parents' room where the sword was kept.

And with it in a flash he ran away.

His dream was still the Knight to slay.

Chapter 2: Incident at an Inn

He stopped that evening at an inn,
But it was filled with ruffians.
A fair young maiden stopped there too.
All eyes were on her, not just a few.

"Hey Lassie!" said one drunken bloke.
And then he told a vulgar joke.
In Celebrier's heart hot anger flamed
To hear a lady so defamed.

He stood up tall. His sword shone bright,
Lit up by the firelight.
"If you would fight me, come and try it!"
The ruffians grew very quiet.

The vulgar fellow turned and fled.

He did not want to lose his head.

The others' hearts were filled with fear,

So they lowered their eyes and drank their beer.

"Thank you, Kind Sir" said the maiden fair.

"I'm so very glad that you were there.

It's hard for a girl to travel alone,

Out in the wild, far from her home."

(The girl he saved was the Royal Princess,

The High King's daughter, nothing less.

She had fled that terrible scene

When the Mad Knight captured the King and Queen.)

Chapter 3: Some Anachronistic Advice

Then a rappin' Minstrel came into the room.

He said, "I wouldn't wanna see you meet your doom.

On any kind of mission, quest, or trip

What a boy like you needs is a Fellowship.

"This job's too big for just you, yourself.

So go and try and find a good-lookin' Elf.

And get a Dwarf too, they're good in fights.

Hey, I'm also thinkin' 'bout the movie rights!"

"Thank you, Sir Minstrel," said Celebrier.

"For the kind advice you gave me here.

Your clever plan would get my vote,

But we're not in the world that Tolkien wrote."

"Hey, it's just my job to give advice.

If you don't like it let's still be nice.

I think you two could give it a try.

But bring along that Lizard/Wizard guy."

Chapter 4: Meeting an Elf and Learning More

The Wizard, now known, took the form of a man

And the three of them sat discussing their plan.

Their voices kept low, their secrets to keep

But an Elf was walking in the forest deep.

He said, "I overheard your plans and am very impressed.

I would be deeply honored to join your quest."

Celebrier said, "More honored we are to have your aid,

But I fear only with suffering will you be paid."

The Elf said, "That's the thing that we Elves love.

It's a chance our virtue to all to prove."

The Wizard said, "How happy our way now seems to go.

But let me ask this moth of the things he does know."

While the others slept the moth talked on

The Wizard listened till they finished at dawn.

He reported, "The Mad Knight is not working alone.

There's an evil Wizard who once turned me to stone.

"He is the one who is controlling the Knight.

So you see the kingdom is in a terrible plight.

And I have more news, and it's really quite dire.

The Bad Wizard's friends with a lady Vampire!

"By day she's so beautiful, so rumors tell,

That all men who see her fall under her spell.

And then every night she turns into a bat.

So I think we'd better watch out for that!"

Chapter 5: Dragon Lore

The Wizard continued, "Our hero needs some magical power,

So the moth told me about midnight hour.

The claw of a Dragon would be just the thing

To overcome evil and get back our King.

"There is a Dragon who might lend us her claw

If we can help her by mending a flaw.

The Vampire cursed her and took away her fire

A solution to that is her most serious desire."

Now the Elf was an expert on Dragon lore.

He had told some and now he told more.

"A female Dragon will not kill you in hate.

Now that makes her very much unlike her mate.

"But you will find you will be just as dead
When a female Dragon takes off your head
Defending her young or defending herself
And that will be that be you man or be Elf.

"Now the answer to this particular woe
Is something the Vampire would certainly know.
We Elves have a potion that forbids one to lie,
If we capture her we could give it a try.

"But what can we offer to appeal to her hate?"
"Oh!" guessed the Princess. "I'm to be bait!
That would be something I'd be willing to do,
To save Mom and Dad. Well, wouldn't you?

"People may think I'm a spoiled young brat,
But there's very much more to me than just that.
I'll do my duty as a Royal Princess.
And when a hero is needed I'll be nothing less.

"Please tell us, Sir Elf, more of your plan.

You'll find I have courage, the same as a man."

(The Elf said, "The Vampire's curse will not affect me,

Because, of course, I'm an Elf as you see.")

Chapter 6: To Capture a Vampire

The Wizard used his shape-shifting power,

Turned into an owl and flew to her tower.

He said, "A Princess I saw alone in the wood.

Does that interest you? I do think it should."

So the Wizard to their trap did lure her

With many more fair words to reassure her.

And soon a bat by the Princess did light

And then it moved forward ready to bite!

Here comes the net! Thrown by the Elf!

A very good throw if he says so himself!

The bat struggles against the net in vain

And when morning comes she's a lady again.

(Celebrier was hid but the others gathered round.

The Wizard now took the form of a hound.)

"Good morning," said the Elf. "This day will be fine.

"Here, have a glass of my Elven wine."

She took a sip of the wine. Well, why not?

And a very good dose of truth potion she got.

"Now," said the Elf. "Please give us the spell

That will make Madam Dragon fiery and well."

She opened her mouth to tell them a lie,

But from her fair lips the true words did fly.

When she saw she had no secrets to keep

She fell to the ground and started to weep.

Hot tears fell too from the Elf-prince's eyes.

A lady's suffering he could not despise.

"Please tell me," he said. "Is there a vow

That you can not break, no matter how?"

And then they witnessed what so few have heard,

A Vampire's oath in their unbreakable word.

She promised her ties to the Bad Wizard to sever

And not to drink men's blood. No, not ever.

She would only drink the blood of the beasts of the farm

And then not enough to do them any harm.

Later that night she flew away home.

No more of her deeds will be told in this poem.

Chapter 7: Interview with a Dragon

The Princess stands by the Dragon's den.

She pauses a moment then she goes in.

"Hello Dear Dragon!" the Princess she calls

And her voice echoes in the cavernous halls.

"I'm very sorry for this awful hex

And really ashamed of the female sex

When I think that a lady, and a smart one too,

Would do such a terrible thing to you.

"I have a potion I'd like you to drink.

It will bring back your fire. What do you think?"

The Dragon emerged from the darkened hall.

She said, "There are so few who call

"On a Dragon. Most rather fear it.

You must have a reason. I'd like to hear it."

"I wouldn't have done it," the Princess she said.

"But my mother and father might both end up dead.

"A mad Knight and bad Wizard have stolen them away,

And a Dragon's claw is needed the villains to slay."

"I see," said the Dragon. "I'll lend a hand.

I'm a mom too and I understand.

"Let's go to your friends this matter to settle.

And may I say I seldom meet someone of your mettle?"

To Celebrier she said, "Strike quickly and cut off my claw.

It will grow back, by natural law."

Chapter 8: Preparing for Battle

The Elf said. "To assault the Bad Tower
Takes more than the power
Of us four, for we are just four.
We need an army and what's more

"We need ladders and engines and slings.
You know, the usual castle-taking things.
Do your parents have friends of the Kings round about?
And if we asked them do you think they'd come out?"

So they went to visit their neighbor King Steven.
He said, "Yes. I would very much like to get even
With this bad Wizard. Now he has kidnapped my friend!
This will be the beginning of his uttermost end!

But Princess, I would like you to marry my son, Prince George,

A closer alliance between our kingdoms to forge."

The Princess said, "Yes. I know this young man.

I think we can make that a part of our plan."

Celebrier's jaw seemed to hit the ground.

His face had the look of a mournful hound.

The Princess said, "Please take that look off your face.

Your feelings for me are so out of place.

"I think you are a most wonderful hero,

But your understanding of true love is just about zero.

I know I'm beautiful, or so I've often been told.

But would you still love me when I'm ugly and old?"

King Steven said, "By royal marriage our kingdoms shall unite!

So let's show our enemies how well we fight!"

He ordered a general conference to be made

And the Vampire came to offer her aid.

When Celebrier looked on that lady dark

His heart leapt with a sudden spark.

And then it was like lightning from heaven above.

And all of his being was filled up with love.

Celebrier's in love with the Lady Vampire!

He said, "For her I would face the worst danger dire.

If I live or I die seems like such a small thing.

Princess, please go on and become the mother of a King."

Celebrier strode up to the Bad Wizard's lair.

He said, "I am the one who can a Dragon's claw wear!

I bid you come out if you dare to fight!

Or else repent and make your evil deeds right!"

The Vampire said, "I've never met a man so brave and so bold,

And I've known many men since I'm really quite old.

All my long life I've stolen men's hearts away.

Now the time has come round where it's my time to pay."

Chapter 9: Happy and Sad Endings

Now of the battle I will let others sing,

For violence and blood are just not my thing.

Victory was won by our heroes bold.

But the Elf fell, as was foretold.

Now my heart is with the Vampire as she sits and waits

For the terrible news that she fears and she hates.

And lo! In the distance! The victors arrive!

Celebrier is with them, wounded but alive.

So she took him to her chamber his injuries to tend

And as over his body she did gracefully bend

She said, "If I bite you, you will become a Vampire."

He said, "That is what I most earnestly desire."

* * *

Since the Vampire was in love her beauty's curse lost its power,

So people could come and visit their tower.

They held many a dinner, party, and dance

With an atmosphere full of joy and romance.

And every night as bats they flew through the air

Over a land both peaceful and fair.

As they danced their bat dance under beautiful stars

The joys of the Universe, they said, "They are ours."

I hope your hankie supply is well

For the Elf's funeral I now will tell.

The Elf's dear body in honor was laid

On a wooden platform by the best carpenters in the two kingdoms made

Out of rosewood for beauty, beech for pure heart, oakwood for giving,

Willow for pity, and pine for hope - in dead Winter still living.

As music to the heavens thrilled

The great hall now with people filled.

A more noble assembly had never been seen.

The two Kings were there, each with his Queen.

And George and the Princess, the royal young pair.

The ideal young couple, said everyone there.

The Wizard arose and spoke these fair words,

While the crowd kept silent so each could be heard.

"Dear friends, we are here to say goodbye to a friend,

But please know that death is never the end

Of a life lived so true and so good

For goodness lives on, that's understood.

"With courage he fought when fighting was his fate.

Though he fought against evil it was never with hate.

To help even his enemies was something he tried."

(With these words the Vampire broke down and cried.)

"As we go on to live

Let us love, let us give.

I promise you this and I promise myself

I'll live my life like my friend the Elf."

The Blue Stone

(About 20 years later.)

Chapter 1: The Blue Stone

Not very long after the old Elf-king departed,
Killing a Dragon (that great-hearted
Elf had stabbed it with a knife,
Saving his friends but losing his life),

The young King sat down with the Queen Mother.
(He was her only child. She had not another.)
She said, "It's never good for a King to reign alone.
The time has now come for you to look in the Stone."

Now, the Elves' Blue Stone was their greatest treasure
And had been for centuries, years beyond measure.
In the depths of its beauty answers could be seen,
And especially what we're talking of, finding a Queen.

So they went to the place where the Stone resided

And so many great questions had been decided.

But like a mighty city by an earthquake shaken

Its casket was broken and the Stone had been taken!

The King set out to recover the Stone

And took two companions, so as to not go alone,

Igor the warrior who some say was insane

And Princess Novita who was his cousin germane.

He said, "There are so many questions. So little we know.

To the wisest person, that's where we should go.

The Good Wizard is he of whom I speak.

He is the one from answers we should seek.

"He serves our neighbor King George in respected station

As Chief Royal Advisor and Minister of Education.

All the day long he gives good advice,

Then he turns into a cat and catches the mice."

Chapter 2: A Royal State Visit

At the palace of George a great feast was prepared.

At the noble guests arriving the common people stared.

Now, you might be wondering and asking, "What is it?"

So, please let me tell you. It's a Royal State Visit.

A more gracious table had seldom been seen.

Novita was seated right next to the Queen.

She said, "Your goodness is known even to us Elves,

How you and your family give of yourselves

"To help make your people happy and good

That's the true way to rule, or anyway it should."

"Thank you," said the Queen. "I credit the King.

He has been most wonderful in everything.

"When our parents saw we responsibility could take

They gave us their crowns and retired to the lake.

And have you met our children, age seventeen?

They are sitting right here, their parents between.

"I only gave birth once, but to our great joy

It was to twins, a girl and a boy."

Prince Eric spoke up (he's the boy twin)

"I'd like to go on a quest, great honor to win."

The Elf-king said, "Our next stop is the Dwarf-king's Hall.

Perhaps you could join us as we give him a call."

Now Anne spoke up (she's the girl as you guessed),

Saying, "Please don't forbid me this quest!

"Now Mother, please listen. When you were my age

You went on an adventure the kingdom to save.

Now the results of that by all can be seen

For the kingdom is saved and you a most wonderful Queen."

The King and the Queen just looked at each other.

The Queen said, "I'm a Queen, yes. But I'm also your mother."

The Wizard coughed and asked to be excused.

He said, "Here's an idea I don't think'll be refused.

"As a Human I've lived far, far too long

But as a beast I'd be still young and strong.

I could go with them the children to protect.

That's something I'm asking with deepest respect."

The King and the Queen agreed with this plan

So the Wizard then asked, "What to be if not man?

I looked at this question and turned it around

And I think I will go as a mighty wolfhound.

"A dog is most useful if you get in a fight

And he can stay up and keep watch at night

And when people get lost, he can find them by smell

And dogs think leftover Human food tastes swell."

Chapter 3: In the Dwarf-king's Hall

On the road one time when they camped for the night

Eric and the Wolfhound stayed up way past the light.

Eric said, "I can remember when we sat in your class.

Me and Anne, a young lad and lass.

"Then you told us of the wonders of the world

And much ancient wisdom to us you unfurled.

I will be glad when we're done with this quest

And be home, the same, and that will be best."

"No," said the Wolfhound. "It shall not be thus.

I've lived my life happily so don't make a fuss.

My Human body grows old and weak.

It passes away now even as we speak.

"Let me tell you something, and please know it's no lie.

If I become Human again it will be only to die.

Now go to bed and please get some rest.

The days ahead will put your strength to the test.

"I will stay up and watch over the camp.

I have a fur coat to keep out the damp."

Soon they reached the Dwarf-king's Hall

And had a big feast. A party for all!

They had roast beef, your choice red or ripe.

The Wolfhound said, "I'll have mine with tripe!"

The Elf-king took the Dwarf-king aside.

He said, "I've got something I'd like to confide.

"Here is the question which I intended:

We've two royal ladies who should by a maid be attended.

Perhaps there's someone who to your household is bound.

I would pay a good price if the right person was found."

"Hmmm," said the Dwarf-king. "It's hard what you say.

We Dwarves have no slaves. That was never our way.

There is one lass in my prison cell.

Grimla's her name. She's known quite well

"For rudeness and getting into fights.

I can free her but can't give you the right

To take her with you against her will.

Nor would she make a good lady's maid with her temper ill."

Grimla was brought into the hall.

Since she was a Dwarf she was not at all tall,

But rather short, plump, and out her chin did shoot.

Still Anne thought she was kind of cute.

(Let me clear up a point that has been kind of weird

By saying just this: Dwarf women don't have beards!)

Grimla was seated at the ladies' table

And given a plate. To eat she was well able.

Novita said, "This roast beef is good, with a slight taste of burn.

That's something we Elves from you Dwarves could learn.

And I really like this multi-mushroom sauce.

And this cute garnish. It looks just like moss."

Picking up an axe she said, "I'd like to learn how this well to throw,

Although I'm considered quite good with a bow.

Still out on a quest it's good to learn more.

You never know what kind of fighting's in store."

Grimla said, "Yes. The secret's in the wrist.

I've thrown many axes at Goblins and not often missed."

The Wolfhound came over. Anne gave him a bone.

He said, "Thanks. One's tastes are one's own."

Grimla gave a start and looked all around.

She said, "I've never heard of a talking hound!"

The Wolfhound said, "Oh that. I'm really a man.

But turned into this. It's all part of a plan.

"But of that I can not say more.

Especially here behind the Dwarven-king's door.

But take it up later with the Elf-king. You'll find he's quite fair,

And even generous when there's treasure to share."

Chapter 4: A Bend in the Road

They left the Dwarves their quest to continue.

When rounding a bend a wonder they did view!

A Dragon lay across the path.

It was sorely wounded, with many a gash.

It turned to them its mighty head,

And slowly, gasping these words said,

"The Spiders have stolen my treasure away.

With my dying breath I on them this curse lay.

"May all their webs be broken and torn,

And their children perish though yet unborn.

May all their dreams come untrue,

And their treasure be lost, copper penny and Elfstone blue.

"May the world be rid of Spiders of giant size.

But not the little ones, the ones that catch flies."

At that our heroes rushed to its side,

But it was too late. The Dragon had died.

The Elf-king said, "I see we are facing a bloody war.

We'll be up to our knees in Spider gore.

There is a chance we'll recover the Stone.

But a much greater chance we will never see home.

"Sir Wolfhound please take the twins back to their land.

They don't belong here. That we all understand.

I will not from their people them take.

Nor will I cause their parents' hearts to break."

"Lady Grimla," he said. "Please give me your answer."

She said, "I've never been a sitter-outer, but a dancer.

It is for friendship and honor that we Dwarves fight.

Ask anyone and he'll tell you I'm right.

"If we prevail and win back the Stone

To have helped a friend will be treasure alone.

And if I die I'll be covered with glory

And be born again in another story."

Chapter 5: Elves and Dragons

They travelled toward the Spiders' headquarters,

A Human castle they had taken over.

On the side of the path..."Hello Elves," said a small lizard.

Novita asked, "Are you a Wizard?"

The lizard just nodded, turned its head to the right,

And then in an instant became a handsome young Knight.

He was dressed head to toe in beautiful mail,

Which shone and shimmered like a serpent's scales.

"It is by happy chance that I here you find.

But I'm not a Wizard nor any of Human kind.

A common enemy we happen to face,

For I am the Prince of the Dragon race.

"You Elves and we Dragons have not often been friends,

As witness your own brave father's unhappy end.

But that kind of thing we should put in the past

So together we can face the Spiders at last.

"They are plotting with their webs to cover all lands

And capture in the strands

All things that live and suck out their blood.

If we can stop that I really think we should.

"I will fight with you in this Human form.

The other Dragons are getting their fires warm.

They will attack from the air

So we can sneak in unaware.

"If we kill their Queen they will lose their spirit.

With that to fight them we shouldn't fear it.

And then we can divide the Spiders' treasure.

The Blue Stone is yours! Well, a part of your measure."

Chapter 6: The Battle is Joined

When they reached the Spiders' stronghold the Dragons
were there.

Black smoke and red flames billowed in the air.

"Come!" said the Dragon-prince. "Follow me in!

The Spiders' last day is about to begin!"

They went in through a hidden side door

And there they faced two dozen Spiders or more.

Many they killed with axe, bow, and sword

But two Spider-guards came toward

The Elf-king and gave him a bite.

That really took him out of the fight!

They took him through a door, which started to close.

The others rushed forward but they were opposed.

Grimla alone made it through the door.

And there she faced a hundred Spiders or more!

She could kill some, but she could not kill all.

And on her from the ceiling wet webs did fall.

They bound her up and took her inside

To an inner chamber and laid her beside

The Elf-king. She struggled against her bonds in vain,

And then fell still with exhaustion and pain.

The Dragon-prince said, "I'm sorry for your Elven-king,

But the fate of all now depends on just one thing.

The Spider-queen we must slay.

You two go while I here stay."

With that he turned to a Dragon grand

And on his four great legs did stand

And lifted up his Dragon tail

And swung it like a mighty flail!

With one blow the wall came down

And all the Spiders gathered round

To kill him or at least to try.

They did not care, live or die.

Dozens he killed with his flames,

But for every one a dozen more came.

Their bodies lay in a terrible stack,

But still they jumped on his wings and back

And gave him many a poison bite

While bravely yet hopelessly he still did fight,

Till at last his strength had passed away

And he perished on that fateful day.

Chapter 7: Endings and Beginnings

The Elf-king awoke. "Grimla," he said. "We may very soon die

As we in the Spiders' captivity lie.

I hope the battle is won as we here abide.

But my feelings for you I will no longer hide.

"I've only loved one woman and she is my mother,

But now I know you I do love another.

I wish we could marry and you reign as my Queen.

Then a happier King would never have been."

Grimla's eyes opened wide as she looked on the King.

She said, "I've never heard a more ridiculous thing.

Your words and your thoughts are like beasts running wild.

Can an Elf and a Dwarf bear a child?

"And what of your people, the Elves so proud?

I don't think a Dwarf-queen would be allowed

To reign over the Elven land,

And that is something you should understand."

The Elf-king said, "If the Elves will not honor you as Queen

The last of them I shall have seen.

I will leave them behind and make a new life

And make a new home with you as my wife."

The Dragons and the Elves won the victory that day,

For the Spider-queen Novita did slay

With a Dwarven axe expertly thrown

And the Elves' treasure was again their own.

"All the rest," said the Elf-king. "You Dragons should

Have, for it's you who gave your precious blood.

A more noble soul I have never known.

Please know you don't shed your tears alone

"For the Dragon-prince who saved us all,

There in the Spiders' terrible hall.

For all Eleven wrongs I'll make amends,

And hope Elves and Dragons will always be friends."

That night under beautiful stars Grimla did stand.

The Elf-king came over and took her by the hand.

She said, "When the Spiders' poison was in your veins

I'm sure that some of it went straight to your brains.

"Those things that you said I hope you forget,

And us on with our lives I hope you let.

An Elf and Dwarf love just never could be.

The idea is quite stupid as I hope you now see."

"No," said the Elf-king. "My heart has now spoken.

And I think also in your heart some feeling has awoken.

Without you I cannot imagine my life.

So I ask you again to be my dear wife."

Of course she said yes and you know the rest.

We all think that true love will be for the best.

Is there a lesson here, for ourselves,

In how a Dwarf lass became Queen of the Elves?

After Words

I hope you enjoyed reading these poems as much as I
enjoyed writing them. If so please check out my more
"serious" poetry book, "Limericks in Love." "The Mad
Knight" and "The Elves' Blue Stone" were written in
2004 as part of my contribution to a group effort on a
JRR Tolkien fan site and recreated from memory in
2022. The opening short poem was written when I was
a teenager. So that was a long time ago.

-Steven Dufour, Walnut Creek, California, USA

Made in the USA
Monee, IL
12 February 2022

91165949R00030